NATIONAL GEOGRAPHIC OUR WORLD

Young Cú Chulainn

Athlete and Future Warrior

◆

Based on a folk tale from Ireland

by Mícheál Ó Súileabháin

NATIONAL GEOGRAPHIC
LEARNING

Long ago, the people of Ireland had a great hero called Cú Chulainn. Cú Chulainn was the son of a god and a human woman.

He was the strongest warrior in the world. When he was just 17, Cú Chulainn defeated whole armies all by himself. He rode in a great chariot, and when he fought he became like a wild animal.

This is the story of how young Cú Chulainn's life as a warrior hero began.

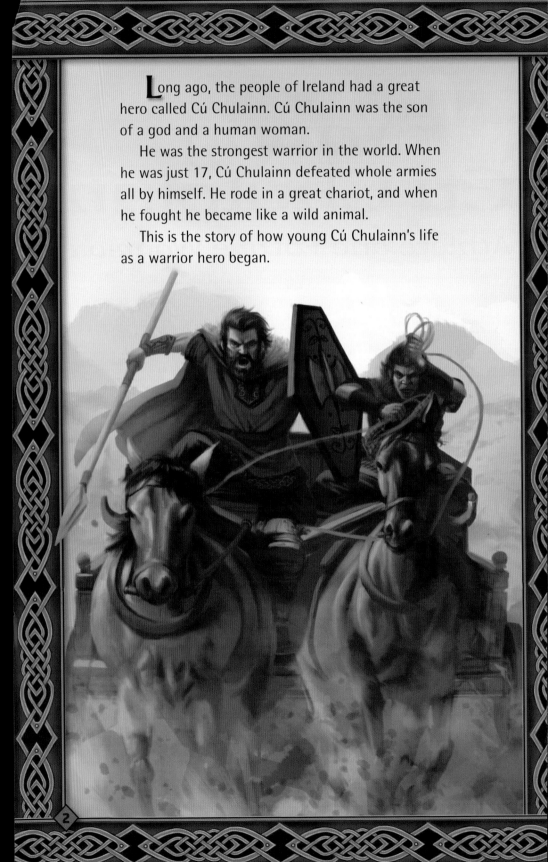

When Cú Chulainn was little, he had another name. His name was Sétanta. Sétanta was not a great warrior yet, but he was a very talented athlete. He practised a sport called hurling, which at the time was the greatest in Ireland.

Hurling is played between two teams on a large field. The only equipment is a wooden stick called a hurley. The players try to hit a hard ball into the other team's goal.

Hurling is an extremely difficult game. And Sétanta was an incredibly skilful hurler, even as a little boy.

When Sétanta was just eight, he practised with his hurley in the fields around his home. He ran like a wild horse. He jumped like a great lion. He had the strength of 20 men.

'Sétanta is so strong and fearless,' said his mother. 'Someday he will be a great warrior.'

And she was right.

One day, Sétanta received a special message that changed his life forever.

One morning while Sétanta was running through the fields, a large bird flew down from the sky.

'Sétanta!' said the magic bird. 'Someday you will be Ireland's greatest warrior hero. That is your destiny.'

The little boy listened carefully to the bird's message.

'But a warrior must have many skills,' Sétanta said. 'I only know how to play hurling.'

'All great Irish warriors start by learning the sport of hurling,' said the bird. 'Then they learn other skills. You can learn those skills, too. The king has got a school for young warriors. Go to that school. Join the boys there and learn to be a warrior!'

Sétanta ran to his house.
He put his clothes in a bag and
picked up his hurley and ball.

'Where are you going?'
asked his mother.

'To the king's school,' he said.
'It is my destiny to be Ireland's
greatest warrior hero.'

'But you are too young to
be with those boys,' said his
mother. 'They are bigger and
older than you!'

But Sétanta was sure of his
destiny. He wanted to start
learning warrior skills now. He
hugged his mother, said goodbye
and ran out of the door.

It only took Sétanta a day to run a hundred miles to the king's school. When he got near the school, he heard many boys playing in the fields. They were playing hurling.

The boys were older and bigger than Sétanta. But he wasn't scared. As soon as he reached the fields, he took his hurley and ran into the game. He didn't even ask for permission to join the boys.

The older boys all looked on with amazement at young Sétanta as he took the hurling ball from the biggest boy. Sétanta caught the ball, ran across the whole field and scored a goal!

'Who is this little child?' asked one of the boys.

'We didn't say he could play with us!' another boy said.

The boys all gathered round Sétanta. They were angry and they wanted to teach the little one a lesson.

The biggest boy walked up to Sétanta and challenged him to a wrestling match. The little hero grabbed the big boy by the arm and threw him over his shoulder. The big boy landed with a thud!

Now the other boys wanted to wrestle Sétanta, too.

'Here we come!' they shouted and they all jumped on Sétanta.

But Sétanta was too strong and quick for the older boys. He started to throw them over his head. They landed on the ground all around him. Soon, each of the older boys had a different injury from trying to wrestle the little hero.

'He's too strong!' one boy said.

'We can't beat him!' cried another.

'This is amazing,' shouted a third boy. 'How can someone so small be so strong?'

When all the boys were lying on the ground, and only Sétanta was still standing, the older boys gave up.

'You win!' they shouted. 'We can't beat you!'

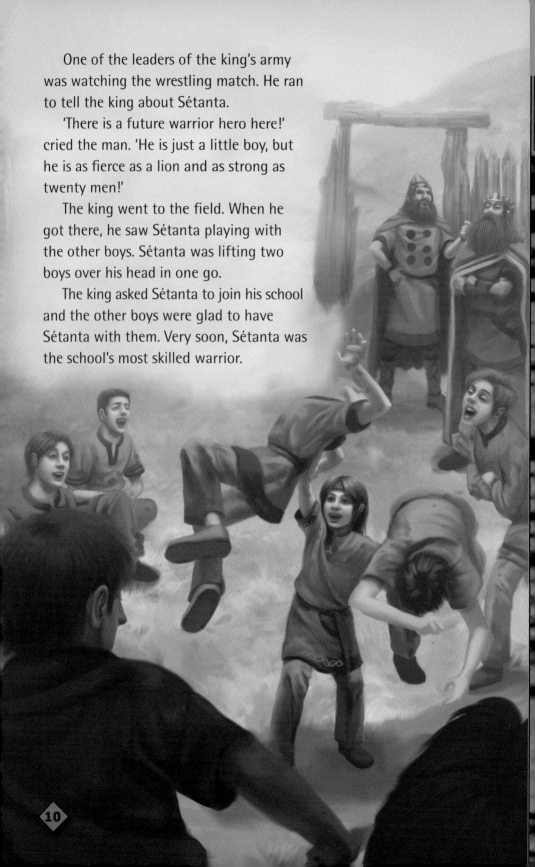

One of the leaders of the king's army was watching the wrestling match. He ran to tell the king about Sétanta.

'There is a future warrior hero here!' cried the man. 'He is just a little boy, but he is as fierce as a lion and as strong as twenty men!'

The king went to the field. When he got there, he saw Sétanta playing with the other boys. Sétanta was lifting two boys over his head in one go.

The king asked Sétanta to join his school and the other boys were glad to have Sétanta with them. Very soon, Sétanta was the school's most skilled warrior.

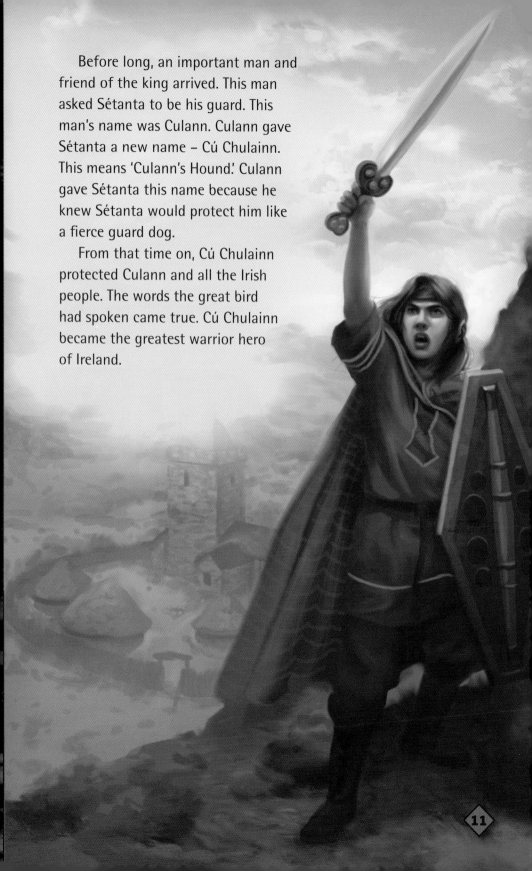

Before long, an important man and friend of the king arrived. This man asked Sétanta to be his guard. This man's name was Culann. Culann gave Sétanta a new name – Cú Chulainn. This means 'Culann's Hound'. Culann gave Sétanta this name because he knew Sétanta would protect him like a fierce guard dog.

From that time on, Cú Chulainn protected Culann and all the Irish people. The words the great bird had spoken came true. Cú Chulainn became the greatest warrior hero of Ireland.

Facts About Incredible Athletes

There have been some incredible athletes in the last 50 years. Many of these athletes became known when they competed in Olympic games. During the Olympics, the best amateur athletes from around the world compete in dozens of different sports. These games may be the greatest test of an athlete's skill. Here are three Olympic athletes who did things no one thought possible.

Nadia Comaneci, Romanian Gymnast

Nadia Comaneci was only 14 years old when she competed in her first Olympics in 1976 in Montreal, Canada. There, Comaneci became the first person to get the highest score possible in gymnastics at the time — a perfect ten. Comaneci, who began training when she was six, won three gold medals at the Montreal Olympics.

Carl Lewis, American Runner

When he was a child, Lewis was a small and skinny boy who was not good at sports. But years of practice and a belief in himself led Lewis to become one of the greatest athletes in the world. He set world records in both running and the long jump, jumping an incredible length of almost 9 metres (29 feet)! Between 1984 and 1996, Lewis won nine Olympic gold medals in jumping and running.

Chen Yanqing, Chinese Weightlifter

Yanqing, who started training when she was 11, was the first woman to win gold medals in women's weightlifting in two Olympic games in a row — both in Athens in 2004 and in Beijing in 2008. This incredibly strong woman has lifted 138 kilograms (304 pounds) — more than twice the weight of her own body!

Word Play Sports

Use the clues to fill in the crossword puzzle with the correct words.

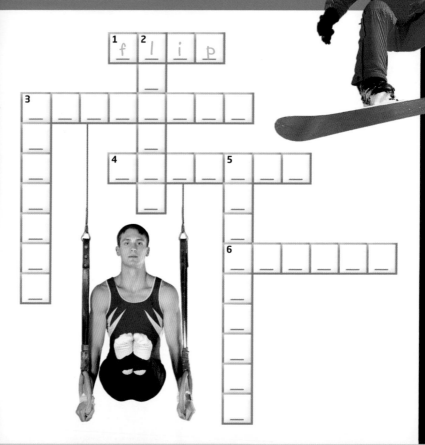

1. f l i p

Across

1. to turn over
3. physical power and energy
4. a person who plays sports
6. damage or harm

Down

2. the measure of something from end to end
3. showing great ability at doing something
5. the items needed for a particular activity

Across: 1. flip; 3. strength; 4. athlete; 6. injury; Down: 2. length; 3. skilful; 5. equipment

Look at the picture. Write a short paragraph about it. Try to use as many of the words below as possible. Use a dictionary if necessary.

athlete   equipment   skilful   strength
land   flip   injury   length

Glossary

amateur doing an activity, such as a sport, without getting paid to do it

armies groups of soldiers who fight together

came true happened as predicted

challenge ask or dare someone to play a game or sport

chariot a wagon with two wheels pulled by one or more horses

defeat beat someone in a game or in a fight

destiny someone's future meant just for that person

fierce wild, strong and powerful

gymnast a person trained in a kind of sport which shows strength, balance and coordination

hero a person who is admired for bravery and accomplishments

leaders people who other people follow

lesson something to be learnt

match a game

message a short written or spoken communication

permission agreement that someone can do something

warrior a person who fights in wars

wrestling the sport of fighting with someone and trying to pin that person down on the ground